# BUTTER IN A LORDLY DISH

by Agatha Christie

samuelfrench.co.uk

ISBN 978-0-573-11687-2

concordtheatricals.co.uk

concordtheatricals.com

www.agathachristielimited.com

---

### FOR PRODUCTION ENQUIRIES

#### UNITED KINGDOM AND WORLD
#### EXCLUDING NORTH AMERICA
licensing@concordtheatricals.co.uk

020-7054-7200

#### UNITED STATES AND CANADA
Info@concordtheatricals.com

1-866-979-0447

Each title is subject to availability from Samuel French,
depending upon country of performance.

---

## MUSIC USE NOTE

## IMPORTANT BILLING AND CREDIT REQUIREMENTS

*BUTTER IN A LORDLY DISH* was first performed on the BBC Radio Light Programme on Tuesday 13 January 1948 and produced by Martyn C. Webster. The cast was as follows:

**SIR LUKE ENDERBY K.C.** . . . . . . . . . . . . . . . . . . . . . . . . . . . . Richard Williams

**LADY ENDERBY**. . . . . . . . . . . . . . . . . . . . . . . . . . . . . . . . . . Lydia Sherwood

**JULIA KEENE** . . . . . . . . . . . . . . . . . . . . . . . . . . . . . . . . . . . . . . Rita Vale

**SUSAN WARREN**. . . . . . . . . . . . . . . . . . . . . . . . . . . . . . . . . . . Thea Wells

**MRS. PETTER** . . . . . . . . . . . . . . . . . . . . . . . . . . . . . . . . . . . . Dora Gregory

**FLORRIE PETTER** . . . . . . . . . . . . . . . . . . . . . . . . . . . . . . . . . . Jill Nyasa

**HAYWARD** . . . . . . . . . . . . . . . . . . . . . . . . . . . . . . . . . . . . . Janet Morrison

**A PORTER**. . . . . . . . . . . . . . . . . . . . . . . . . . . . . . . . . . . . David Kossoff

# CHARACTERS

SIR LUKE ENDERBY K.C.

LADY ENDERBY

JULIA KEENE

SUSAN WARREN

MRS. PETTER

FLORRIE PETTER

HAYWARD

A PORTER

## Scene One

*(The confused noises of a London street are heard. "Star," "Standard," "The News." A distant door opens and bangs and street noise fade.* **FLORRIE** *calls in a clear cockney accent.)*

**FLORRIE.** Hi, Mums?

**MRS. PETTER.** That you, Florrie?

**FLORRIE.** Yes.

*(A door opens.)*

**MRS. PETTER.** Hello dear.

**FLORRIE.** *(Sniffs.)* Is my nose telling me there's somethin' good for tea?

**MRS. PETTER.** Fish and chips.

**FLORRIE.** H'm, good.

*(The door closes.)*

Oh drat! What's all these suitcases doing here? Doesn't half clutter the place up.

**MRS. PETTER.** It's Mrs. Keene's things.

**FLORRIE.** Oh, the lodger. She going away?

**MRS. PETTER.** Yes, but she's not going to take these with her – only one small case.

**FLORRIE.** Why?

**MRS. PETTER.** Because she's not certain yet where she'll be. She'll let us know where she wants all this sent.

**FLORRIE.** Seems peculiar to me – going away and not knowing where she's going.

**MRS. PETTER.** What do you mean?

**FLORRIE.** I'll bet she's off for the weekend with someone.

**MRS. PETTER.** Now don't talk like that. It's not nice.

**FLORRIE.** All right, but if you ask me, there's something fishy about our Mrs. Keene.

**MRS. PETTER.** Now stop it, Florrie. She's a very nice lady. Always speaks so pleasant.

**FLORRIE.** That's the kind that gets things from shops without paying for them. Confidence tricksters, they call them. Mind she pays you before she waltzes off.

**MRS. PETTER.** She has paid me, right up to tomorrow and a bit over for leaving the cases and sending them on. So you ought to be ashamed of yourself for being so suspicious.

**FLORRIE.** All right – but I know what I know.

**MRS. PETTER.** What do you know?

**FLORRIE.** Well, it was last week. I was going along from Park Lane into Berkeley Square and there was a party on at one of those big houses, you know, cocktails and sherry and all that.

**MRS. PETTER.** Well!

**FLORRIE.** Well, who should I see coming out with a tall, handsome man but our Mrs. Keene. Dressed up to the nines, fox furs and one of those flyaway black velvet hats. I will say she looked a treat, but it's odd, you'll admit.

**MRS. PETTER.** What?

**FLORRIE.** Going to swell society houses all dressed up and lodging here with us just off the Pimlico Road. It doesn't fit, somehow.

**MRS. PETTER.** And I suppose you've got some far-fetched notion to account for it.

**FLORRIE.** If you ask me, she's in with one of those gangs of society burglars.

**MRS. PETTER.** The nonsense you talk.

**FLORRIE.** She goes along to places and finds out where the stuff is kept, and when the house is likely to be empty, and passes the word on to the gang.

**MRS. PETTER.** And if you ask me, you go too much to the pictures! Gangs, indeed!

**FLORRIE.** Well, gangs aren't only on at the pictures. You read about them in the newspapers, too.

**MRS. PETTER.** Nonsense.

**FLORRIE.** Come off it, Mum, you like a nice little bit of crime yourself.

**MRS. PETTER.** Talking of crime, is that an evening paper you've got there?

**FLORRIE.** Yes.

**MRS. PETTER.** Is the verdict out on that taxi driver case?

**FLORRIE.** No, not yet. Just the judge's summing up.

**MRS. PETTER.** Oh!

**FLORRIE.** You know, I don't see what use judges are. They don't seem to say anything useful or tell the jury what they ought to do.

**MRS. PETTER.** How'd you mean?

**FLORRIE.** Well, listen to this, "Whereas Sir Luke has stated in the case for the prosecution", etcetera, etcetera, "In which case the prisoner is undoubtedly guilty – but at the same time you must take into account the contention of the defence, that the prisoner had not the necessary knowledge to," etcetera, etcetera, "In which case you will have no alternative but to acquit the accused." Why doesn't he tell them if the prisoner's done it or not?

**MRS. PETTER.** Perhaps he doesn't know.

**FLORRIE.** Well, he's the judge, isn't he? Fancy if you had weather forecasts like that.

*(She speaks in an exaggerated voice.)*

If the weather improves tomorrow, it will be warm and sunny. If, on the other hand, the depression spreads, it will be wet and cold.

**MRS. PETTER.** Might as well have a weather forecast like that, for all the good they are. Ruined my best hat last Sunday, listening to what they said.

**FLORRIE.** Now, I like a man like Sir Luke Enderby, the one who was prosecuting. Gave it to the jury hot and strong, he did. Beautiful it was, especially that bit about doing their duty, however painful, and how people like the prisoner were a menace to society.

**MRS. PETTER.** I remember Sir Luke Enderby in that blonde on the beach murder.

**FLORRIE.** Yes, that's the man.

**MRS. PETTER.** All about those poor girls being lured to their death by a sadistic murderer. That was a good murder, that was. I don't like this taxi murder so much.

**FLORRIE.** No, it's a bit dull.

**MRS. PETTER.** But of course, he did it all right.

**FLORRIE.** Yes, but he looks such an insignificant little chap. Now Garfield, the blonde on the beach murderer, he was really good looking.

**MRS. PETTER.** Now you be careful, Florrie.

**FLORRIE.** Why?

**MRS. PETTER.** That's what all those poor girls thought – they let him pick them up as easy as easy. You be careful of these flash, good looking fellows that try to pick girls up.

*(A knock at the door is heard.)*

**FLORRIE.** That must be Mrs. Keene.

*(She calls.)*

Come in!

*(The door opens. **JULIA** speaks in a charming voice.)*

**JULIA.** Good evening, Mrs. Petter.

**MRS. PETTER.** Good evening, Mrs. Keene.

**JULIA.** Good evening, Florrie.

**FLORRIE.** Evening.

**JULIA.** I wonder if I might use your telephone Mrs. Petter?

**MRS. PETTER.** Why, certainly, Mrs. Keene. Come in.

**JULIA.** Thank you.

**MRS. PETTER.** Do you want the book?

**JULIA.** No, I know the number.

(*There is a slight pause.*)

It isn't foggy outside, is it, Florrie?

**FLORRIE.** Just a bit – not much.

(**JULIA** *is heard dialling.*)

**JULIA.** It will be all right in the country, I hope.

**MRS. PETTER.** You going to the country?

**JULIA.** Just for the weekend.

**MRS. PETTER.** Well, I'll just – come on, Florrie.

(*The door closes.*)

**JULIA.** Hullo? Is that nineteen Chishold Gardens?... Can I speak to Sir Luke Enderby please?... Oh, I see... No, no message... No name...

(*Her voice fades as we flip to the other side of the call.*)

I'll ring again later...

(*There is a click as* **HAYWARD** *replaces the receiver. His voice is elderly and rather gloomy.*)

**HAYWARD.** No message. No name. She'll ring again later. Another of them!

(*The front door bell is heard ringing.*)

There's the front door. First the telephone, then the door! If it's not one thing, it's another.

(*The front door opens and the sound of a London residential square is heard.* **SUSAN** *is a brisk young woman with an astringent manner.*)

**SUSAN.** Good afternoon, Hayward.

**HAYWARD.** Good afternoon, Miss Warren.

*(The front door closes.)*

**HAYWARD.** Lady Enderby isn't in yet, but she's expecting you.

**SUSAN.** Oh, that's all right. Sir Luke's still at the Old Bailey, I suppose?

**HAYWARD.** Yes madam, will you come in to the drawing room?

> *(There is a slight pause. They are heard moving through the house.)*

**SUSAN.** How's the rheumatism, Hayward?

**HAYWARD.** It's been bad lately, what with the telephone and answering the door.

**SUSAN.** Oh I'm sorry.

**HAYWARD.** These large houses are very inconvenient. I said to her ladyship only yesterday, how different it would be if we could have a nice flat.

**SUSAN.** A nice flat wouldn't take all Lady Enderby's nice things.

**HAYWARD.** Ye-e-es, her ladyship has got some nice things. She's out at the sale rooms this afternoon.

**SUSAN.** Oh, so that's where she is! There'll be even more lovely things presently. No hope of that nice flat, Hayward.

**HAYWARD.** No.

**SUSAN.** It's more likely to be an even larger house.

**HAYWARD.** Oh, don't suggest that, madam. Would you care for the evening paper?

**SUSAN.** No thanks. I'll amuse myself with a book.

**HAYWARD.** Right, madam.

**SUSAN.** What's this one? *Ogden on Criminal Jurisprudence.* That's Sir Luke's, I suppose.

**HAYWARD.** Yes.

**SUSAN.** A bit heavy for me.

> *(The front door opens and closes. Someone is heard approaching.)*

HAYWARD. That's either her ladyship or Sir Luke.

SIR LUKE. Well, well, look who's here!

SUSAN. Hello Luke.

SIR LUKE. Lovely to see you, Susan. Where's Marion?

SUSAN. At the sale rooms.

SIR LUKE. That will mean more Buhl cabinets and Aubusson carpets and Chinese bronzes! *(Quietly.)* Any telephone messages for me, Hayward?

HAYWARD. A lady rang up just now, sir. She didn't leave her name or a message.

*(SIR LUKE speaks rather falsely.)*

SIR LUKE. I wonder who that could be.

SUSAN. *(Ironically.)* I suppose you couldn't possibly guess.

HAYWARD. Shall I bring in tea, sir?

SIR LUKE. Yes, please.

HAYWARD. Thank you, sir.

*(The door closes softly.)*

SUSAN. Do you encourage them to ring you up here?

SIR LUKE. I don't know what you mean!

SUSAN. Come off it, darling. I mean your various lady friends.

SIR LUKE. Aren't you well aware, Susan, that you're the only girl I've ever loved?

SUSAN. I'm aware that you're never at a loss for an answer! How did the case go?

SIR LUKE. The case?

SUSAN. Haven't you just come from the Old Bailey?

SIR LUKE. Oh, that. Guilty. Couldn't have been any other verdict. Why the jury wanted to stay out two hours and a half, I can't imagine.

SUSAN. No indeed. After your masterly speech the jury should have brought him in guilty without bothering to leave the box!

SIR LUKE. After all, he did shoot the taxi driver.

**SUSAN.** Yes, I can't pretend there has really been a grave miscarriage of justice, although I always try to.

**SIR LUKE.** Why?

**SUSAN.** Just to annoy you.

**SIR LUKE.** Why do you want to get your knife into me? What have I done to you?

**SUSAN.** Nothing. You just look so completely sure of yourself and so thoroughly pleased with yourself!

(*The front door opens and closes. Someone is heard approaching.*)

**MARION.** Darlings, am I terribly late?

**SUSAN.** How are you, Marion?

**MARION.** Susan dear, how nice to see you.

(*The chinking of a tea tray is heard.*)

Why on earth didn't you start tea? Oh good, Hayward's bringing it now.

**SIR LUKE.** (*Quietly.*) Were there any letters for me, Hayward?

**HAYWARD.** In your study, sir.

**SIR LUKE.** I'd better just have a look at them.

(*The door closes.*)

**MARION.** Milk, Susan? You don't have sugar, I know.

**SUSAN.** Thank you.

**MARION.** I hope you haven't been waiting very long?

**SUSAN.** Oh no, I've been improving my mind with this book.

**MARION.** (*Amused.*) My goodness, not *Criminal Jurisprudence*?

**SUSAN.** Does Luke really read this sort of thing for pleasure?

**MARION.** Not exactly pleasure. Just to look up some special point.

**SUSAN.** I know the sort of thing. Doublechuck v. Fathead in the reign of Charles the First – and for some inscrutable reason it affects the case of the Crown v. Dreary Product Limited today. I really think the law is extraordinary!

**MARION.** I must say that sometimes it doesn't seem very sensible. Bread and butter, dear?

**SUSAN.** Thanks.

*(There is a slight pause.)*

Luke's looking frightfully pleased with himself.

**MARION.** I suppose the verdict was guilty. He said it was a certainty.

**SUSAN.** Naturally. He was just slightly annoyed at the jury being impertinent enough to stay out two hours and a half. Lèse majesté after his speech for the prosecution.

**MARION.** *(Hurt.)* Susan darling, that's not very kind.

**SUSAN.** Darling, it was abominable of me. But I would simply hate to stand in the dock charged with murder and have Luke prosecuting.

**MARION.** But you'd like it if he were defending you?

**SUSAN.** Perhaps. But he never does seem to defend people.

**MARION.** Well anyway, if you were innocent, you'd have nothing to be afraid of.

**SUSAN.** Wouldn't I?

**MARION.** Innocent people are always acquitted.

**SUSAN.** Are they? I wonder.

**MARION.** Of course.

**SUSAN.** I wish I was as sure about it as you are.

*(The door opens.)*

**MARION.** Ask Luke.

**SIR LUKE.** Ask Luke what?

**SUSAN.** Are innocent people always acquitted?

**SIR LUKE.** No need to worry about that. The real worry is that some cold-blooded murderer gets off scot-free because some sentimental women on the jury like his face.

**SUSAN.** The blonde on the beach? Garfield?

**MARION.** But he wasn't acquitted.

**SIR LUKE.** No, but he might have been. There were four women on the jury.

**SUSAN.** Extraordinary how women fell for that man. How many women had he actually killed?

**SIR LUKE.** Certainly two –

**SUSAN.** The original blonde at Bexhill and that girl at Weymouth?

**SIR LUKE.** Probably three – and possibly a good many more!

**SUSAN.** He was terribly good looking. Mad, I suppose?

**SIR LUKE.** Oh no, not in the legal sense. He knew what he was doing all right.

**MARION.** *(Plaintively.)* Couldn't you two possibly stop talking about murders?

**SIR LUKE.** Sorry, darling. Tell me what you've been doing? Sotheby's?

**MARION.** Christie's. My dears, I got the most lovely pair of Chinese pictures on glass. Absolutely exquisite.

**SIR LUKE.** And where are you going to put them?

**MARION.** I'm going to hang them on that wall over there. There were a lot of dealers after them – they ran me up rather high.

**SIR LUKE.** Just as well I make a bit at the bar.

**SUSAN.** You hang people and Marion hangs pictures!

**MARION.** But they really are unique.

**SUSAN.** So is this house – absolutely perfect, darling.

**SIR LUKE.** It should be, when you consider that Marion's house comes first, and Marion's husband a long way after.

**MARION.** What nonsense! I'm the most devoted wife.

**SIR LUKE.** You're the most wonderful wife a man ever had.

**SUSAN.** Twitter, twitter, coo coo! Listen to the turtledoves – excuse my vulgar noises.

**MARION.** More tea, Luke?

**SIR LUKE.** No time. I must be off. Got to catch a train to Liverpool.

**SUSAN.** Why Liverpool?

**SIR LUKE.** Work to be done.

**MARION.** Oh, what a bore. Really, dear, you ought to have some time off. You work much too hard.

**SIR LUKE.** I'll have a real rest one of these days. Goodbye, darling, take care of yourself.

**MARION.** Bye, dear.

**SIR LUKE.** Bye, Susan. Be good.

**SUSAN.** Wouldn't that come better from me to you?

**SIR LUKE.** Now then Susan. I must run. I'll miss my train.

> *(There is a pause. The front door bangs closed.* **SUSAN***'s tone changes completely.)*

**SUSAN.** Gone to meet some woman, I suppose?

> *(All the brightness vanishes from* **MARION***'s voice. It sounds dead and tired.)*

**MARION.** Probably.

**SUSAN.** How you stand it I don't know, Marion.

**MARION.** After a time one doesn't mind so much.

**SUSAN.** I wonder. How long have you been married?

**MARION.** Ten years.

**SUSAN.** And practically all the time Luke has been chasing after some woman or other?

**MARION.** Oh, not on the honeymoon. I think he was absolutely faithful on the honeymoon.

**SUSAN.** That's very nearly the most cutting thing I've ever heard you say! Haven't you ever considered leaving him?

**MARION.** I've considered it, yes.

**SUSAN.** Tell me, do you care for him still?

**MARION.** Oh my dear, so many things go to make up a marriage. There are the boys. They're devoted to him and he's an excellent father. And he is always kind and charming to me. I think he's really very fond of me. All those women don't really mean anything, you know. These infatuations never last. It's just – well – weakness on his part. Any good looking woman has only to throw herself at his head and he accepts the challenge.

**SUSAN.** Whose challenge is he accepting at this minute?

**MARION.** I think this is a new one. By all the signs.

**SUSAN.** Any idea who she is?

**MARION.** None at all.

**SUSAN.** I wonder where they're meeting? Certainly not Liverpool. I wonder...

(*Fade.*)

## Scene Two

*(The noises of a train station are heard.)*

**FIRST VOICE.** Could you tell me what platform for Henley?

**SECOND VOICE.** I'm sorry I've no idea. Perhaps a porter could help you.

**THIRD VOICE.** Could you manage a corner seat?

**PORTER.** Well, I'll try but we're pretty full up.

**SIR LUKE.** Julia, dearest! You've really come! I was so afraid you wouldn't.

*(JULIA's voice is deep with emotion.)*

**JULIA.** What a wonderful place Paddington Station is. I never realised it before.

**SIR LUKE.** Julia...

**JULIA.** I telephoned, but you weren't in.

**SIR LUKE.** I heard someone had rung up. I was terrified that it was to say you'd changed your mind.

**JULIA.** As if I would.

**SIR LUKE.** Oh Julia, how beautiful you are. I do love you!

**JULIA.** *(Shakily.)* You can't say things like that in Paddington Station. Besides we shall miss our train.

**SIR LUKE.** I don't even know where we're going.

**JULIA.** That makes it more exciting, doesn't it? Come along, we must hurry. It's number five.

**SIR LUKE.** Where are we going?

**JULIA.** The station's called Warning Halt.

**SIR LUKE.** Warning Halt? Never heard of it.

**JULIA.** Nobody has. Come on, hurry.

**SIR LUKE.** It sounds completely the back of beyond.

**JULIA.** Oh, we'll miss the train. Run!

**PORTER.** Stand away there!

*(A train is heard whistling and puffing smoke as it pulls out of the station. Fade.)*

## Scene Three

*(The screech of brakes is heard as the train draws into a country platform.)*

PORTER. *(Calling.)* Warning Halt, Warning Halt.

JULIA. Thank goodness, no fog here.

SIR LUKE. Yes, thank goodness. Do we get a taxi?

JULIA. Oh no, we walk. My cottage is only about three minutes away.

PORTER. Tickets, please. Thank you. Good evening.

JULIA. Good evening. No, this way – there's a footpath across the field.

SIR LUKE. Oh, it's a heavenly night. Just look at those clouds chasing each other across the moon.

JULIA. Come on, you old poet. It's too cold to stand stargazing.

SIR LUKE. You know, I never knew you had a cottage in the country.

JULIA. But then you don't know much about me, do you?

SIR LUKE. I know that when I saw you across the room at the Ritz that day, and you smiled at me, that the whole world changed. Just over a fortnight ago. It seems a lifetime. And now, at last –

JULIA. Dearest, you don't mind, do you, coming here to the cottage? I did so hate the idea of a hotel for us. It seemed so sordid – the subterfuges, false names, perhaps meeting someone who might recognise us. Oh, I couldn't bear it. You do understand, don't you?

SIR LUKE. Of course I do, dearest. I love you even more for being so sensitive. All that matters is that we should be together. I don't care how primitive the place is.

JULIA. *(Playfully.)* I'd have you know that my cottage is not primitive. It has every creature comfort. Hot water and electric light, and to cheer us through the beastly rationing, the best to eat that the local black market can provide.

SIR LUKE. Ha, sounds wonderful.

*(Fade.)*

## Scene Four

*(The sound of* JULIA *searching her handbag for keys.)*

JULIA. Here we are. Let me find the key. I've got it.

*(The front door unlocks.)*

Just a minute. I'll switch on the light. There, how do you like my retreat?

SIR LUKE. It's delightful. What a charming room.

*(The door closes.)*

JULIA. I hoped you'd like it. Just set a match to the fire. I'll bring in supper. It's all ready.

*(A match strikes and the fire begins to crackle.)*

SIR LUKE. What a wonderful woman you are, Julia. Even your fire lights and burns up at once. Isn't that supposed to be a sign that your lover is true to you? What a lovely thing a fire is on an autumn evening.

*(He calls.)*

Julia?

JULIA. *(Offstage.)* Coming!

SIR LUKE. *(Calling.)* You're a wonderful woman.

JULIA. *(Offstage.)* What? Here we are.

*(The sound of dishes being put on a table is heard.)*

What were you saying?

SIR LUKE. *(Ardently.)* That you're the most wonderful creature in the world. There's something different about you from any other woman I've ever met.

JULIA. *(Mockingly.)* And how many women have you said that to?

SIR LUKE. *(Amorously.)* Darling...

**JULIA.** No, no, Luke. Be good. Supper. Definitely supper, and though I say it myself, rather a good supper.

**SIR LUKE.** By Jove, cold duck. And is that pâté?

**JULIA.** It is.

**SIR LUKE.** And do my eyes deceive me, is that immense yellow pyramid real butter?

(**JULIA** *speaks in a rather peculiar voice.*)

**JULIA.** Butter in a lordly dish...

**SIR LUKE.** *(Gaily.)* It sounds quite Biblical.

**JULIA.** Does it? *(Gravely.)* Is my lord satisfied with what his servant has set before him?

**SIR LUKE.** *(Amorously.)* You enchanting creature. Julia...

**JULIA.** *(Playfully.)* No, not now. Supper. I insist on stern self-control till after supper.

*(They both laugh. Fade.)*

## Scene Five

*(The fire is heard blazing.)*

**JULIA.** Now then, sit in the big armchair. I'll put your coffee by you here.

**SIR LUKE.** Oh darling. What a perfect meal that was. And now, perfect coffee! Damned few women can make good coffee. It seems incredible, Julia, that a fortnight ago I'd never even seen you.

**JULIA.** I've known you by sight a much longer time. You were pointed out to me.

**SIR LUKE.** Really?

**JULIA.** You're a very celebrated man.

**SIR LUKE.** Nonsense.

**JULIA.** You're the most famous counsel in England. Doesn't it ever upset you to feel that your eloquence and your power has got some poor wretch hanged?

**SIR LUKE.** Not if the poor wretch richly deserves it.

**JULIA.** Supposing he doesn't? Supposing he's innocent?

**SIR LUKE.** I don't think that what you so romantically call, my eloquence, or my legal tricks, have ever hanged an innocent man.

**JULIA.** No.

**SIR LUKE.** There's not usually much doubt about murderers who get convicted. Trouble is that occasionally a fellow gets off who's as guilty as hell.

**JULIA.** Garfield didn't get off...

**SIR LUKE.** The blonde on the beach murderer?

**JULIA.** Yes.

**SIR LUKE.** Oh, no doubt about him.

**JULIA.** But supposing he wasn't guilty. There wasn't really very much evidence against him, was there?

**SIR LUKE.** My dear girl, the police had been after Garfield for months. There had been two other girls before that, remember. The police knew quite well who had done it, but I believe his wife always cooked up the most wonderful alibi for him. Not that a wife's word goes very far – but in the absence of definite evidence of his having been seen with the girls near the times of the murders, they couldn't risk charging him before.

JULIA. That's what I say. There wasn't really any evidence against him.

SIR LUKE. Now look here, Julia, talking strict facts – not legal tender – but plain, off the record, common sense.

JULIA. Well.

SIR LUKE. Garfield is friendly with girl number one. She's strangled. Garfield has a date with girl number two. She's found dead. Then he carries on with girl number three and she's murdered. Can't be coincidence. The fellow's got a sex complex and can't resist killing these girls.

JULIA. Then why didn't they say he was insane?

SIR LUKE. Because he wasn't. He knew well enough what he was doing and what would happen to him if he got caught. And he was so extraordinarily clever that it wasn't easy to catch him.

JULIA. The judge's summing up was in his favour.

SIR LUKE. Ye-e-s, the actual evidence was thin. But it wasn't needed. The jury took one look at Garfield and made up their minds.

JULIA. No, they listened to you. You got him convicted.

SIR LUKE. Well, perhaps I did my bit. He was a nice looking chap. A plausible way with him. Couple of women on the jury were looking quite sentimental about him. I had to smash that.

JULIA. Women have very sound instincts.

SIR LUKE. Now don't give me that old stuff about a woman's instinct. Women are notorious for liking wrong 'uns. Look at that wife of his. Blindly devoted to him, apparently. If she hadn't been in hospital with typhoid at the time of the trial, she might somehow have pulled the trick again. I never saw her, but I believe she was an amazingly good liar – or so Inspector Garrod told me. When she swore to him that Garfield had been at home with her at the crucial times, you couldn't help but believe her. Amazing creatures, women.

*(He gives a sharp exclamation of pain.)*

**JULIA.** What's the matter?

**SIR LUKE.** Ooh – got cramp in my leg. Ah, that's better.

**JULIA.** Have some more coffee.

**SIR LUKE.** Thank you, darling. What a meal! You're a wonderful woman, Julia. "Butter in a lordly dish" – now where does that come from? The Bible? Esther? No, it isn't Esther.

**JULIA.** Don't you remember?

**SIR LUKE.** I'll get it in a minute.

*(He gives another exclamation of pain.)*

Ooh – funny this cramp. I feel quite stiff. What were we talking about?

**JULIA.** Killing...

**SIR LUKE.** Oh, yes. Garfield. If that man had been able to leave women alone, he'd be alive today.

**JULIA.** But some men can't leave women alone, can they? *(Significantly.)* Can they, Luke?

**SIR LUKE.** I'm fond of women, I admit it. But this time, with you, it's something quite different.

**JULIA.** Yes, one always has to say that. It's expected. What does your wife feel about these excursions of yours?

**SIR LUKE.** *(Cautiously.)* I think we'd better leave my wife out of it.

**JULIA.** I'm sorry.

*(There is a pause.)*

**SIR LUKE.** "Butter in a lordly dish" – funny how that keeps running in my mind. Why do I feel those words have got a – a kind of sinister sound to them? I wish I could remember.

**JULIA.** Would these help you to remember?

**SIR LUKE.** I can't see what it is you're holding up there. What's the matter with my eyes? I can't focus properly.

**JULIA.** It's a hammer and some nails.

**SIR LUKE.** *(Amused.)* You extraordinary woman. What do you want a hammer and nails for?

**JULIA.** Perhaps to hang up a picture on the wall.

**SIR LUKE.** At this time of night? Really, Julia, what a barbarous idea!

**JULIA.** Yes, it is rather barbarous. But then women can be barbarous.

(*There is a pause.*)

It was, of course, a grave breach of hospitality.

**SIR LUKE.** What was?

**JULIA.** What Jael did to Sisera.

**SIR LUKE.** Jael? Sisera? Of course, I've got it! Jael and Sisera. She's the one who brought him butter in a lordly dish and then hammered a nail through his forehead.

(*His voice changes suddenly.*)

A nail...

**JULIA.** What's the matter, Luke?

**SIR LUKE.** *(Thickly.)* I – look here – damn, I'm stiff and cramped all over. My eyes are playing me tricks – all misty. I can't get up!

**JULIA.** No, you can't get up. That's the result of the drug in your coffee.

**SIR LUKE.** Drug in the coffee? What do you mean, Julia?

**JULIA.** The drug I put in your coffee. Do you know who I am, Luke?

**SIR LUKE.** You're Julia.

**JULIA.** Julia, yes. But my other name?

**SIR LUKE.** Keene. Julia Keene.

**JULIA.** No, I took the name of Keene. My own name was rather too conspicuous. I'm Julia Garfield, Luke.

**SIR LUKE.** What? Garfield... Garfield?!

**JULIA.** I'm Henry Garfield's wife. That is, I should be Henry Garfield's wife – but for you. Because of you and your eloquence and your legal tricks, I'm Henry Garfield's widow.

**SIR LUKE.** *(Drowsily.)* What's all this? What are you up to?... You got me here...

**JULIA.** It wasn't very difficult. I knew your reputation. You fall for women very easily, don't you, Luke?

**SIR LUKE.** I – must – get – out – of – here –

**JULIA.** I loved Henry Garfield.

**SIR LUKE.** I – must – get – out – of – here!

**JULIA.** I loved Henry Garfield. You killed him.

**SIR LUKE.** Henry Garfield was – a murderer –

**JULIA.** Oh no, he wasn't. I killed those women.

**SIR LUKE.** You?

**JULIA.** It wasn't Henry's fault. He just fell easily for women – like you. They beckoned and he followed. But I wasn't like your wife, content to sit at home and buy pretty things and shut her eyes. I wasn't going to share Henry with any woman – silly, giggling little blondes! They didn't giggle when I'd finished with them.

>    (**JULIA** *laughs darkly.*)

**SIR LUKE.** Stop that.

**JULIA.** Yes, I must stop it. There are things to do.

**SIR LUKE.** You're mad... You're mad!

**JULIA.** *(Calmly.)* Not in the legal sense. I know quite well what I'm going to do.

**SIR LUKE.** *(Frenzied.)* Put that hammer down – go away from me! God, I can't move! Keep away from me! Marion... Marion...! Keep her away from me! Keep away... Keep away...!

>    (*A groan is heard. There is a slight pause then the sound of a nail being hammered into something soft.* **JULIA** *laughs madly.*)

**End of Play**

# THE AGATHA CHRISTIE COLLECTION

Agatha Christie is regarded as the most successful female playwright of all time. Her illustrious dramatic career spans forty-two years, countless acclaimed original plays, several renowned novels adapted for stage, and numerous collections of thrilling one-act plays. Testament to Christie's longevity, these plays continue to engage great artists and enthral audiences today.

Since the première of her first play in 1930 the world of theatre has changed immeasurably, and so has the way plays are published and performed. Embarking upon a two-year project, Agatha Christie Limited sought to re-open Christie's distinguished body of dramatic work, looking to both original manuscripts and the most recent publications to create a "remastered" edition of each play. Each new text would contain only the words of Agatha Christie (or adaptors she personally worked with) and all extraneous materials that might come between the interpreter and the playwright would be removed, ultimately bringing the flavor and content of the texts closer to what the author would have delivered to the rehearsal room. Each new edition would then be specifically tailored to the needs and requirements of the professional twenty-first century artist.

The result is The Collection.

Whether in a classic revival or new approach, The Collection has been purposely assembled for the contemporary theatre professional. The choice and combination of plays offers something for all tastes and kinds of performance with the skill, imagination and genius of Agatha Christie's work now waiting to be explored anew in theatre.

For more information on The Collection, please visit
agathachristielimited.com/licensing/stage/browse-by-play

Lightning Source UK Ltd.
Milton Keynes UK
UKHW051235090120
356600UK00015B/634/P

9 780573 116872